Ten Poe
about Black H

ex libris

Candlestick Press

Published by:

Candlestick Press,
Diversity House, 72 Nottingham Road, Arnold, Nottingham NG5 6LF
www.candlestickpress.co.uk

Design and typesetting by Craig Twigg

Printed by Ratcliff & Roper Print Group, Nottinghamshire, UK

Selection and Introduction © Panya Banjoko, 2022

Cover illustration © Morag Williams, 2022
Instagram @moragwilliamsart

Candlestick Press monogram © Barbara Shaw, 2008

© Candlestick Press, 2022

ISBN 978 1 907598 88 3

Acknowledgements

The poems in this pamphlet are reprinted from the following books, all by
permission of the publishers listed unless stated otherwise. Every effort has been
made to trace the copyright holders of the poems published in this book. The
editor and publisher apologise if any material has been included without
permission or without the appropriate acknowledgement, and would be glad to be
told of anyone who has not been consulted.

Thanks are due to all the copyright holders cited below for their kind permission:

Stanley O. Ayodeji, *After the Riot, Quiet!* (Createspace Independent Publishing
Platform, 2014) by kind permission of the author. Panya Banjoko, poem first
published in this anthology, by kind permission of the author. James Berry,
Fractured Circles (New Beacon Books, 1979) by kind permission of Myra Barrs
© The Estate of James Berry. Jean 'Binta' Breeze, *Third World Girl: Selected
Poems, with Live DVD* (Bloodaxe Books, 2011) www.bloodaxebooks.com.
Kamau Brathwaite, poem appeared in *Writing Black Britain 1948-1998: An
Interdisciplinary Anthology* ed. James Proctor (Manchester University Press,
2000) by kind permission of the Estate of Kamau Brathwaite. Len Garrison,
Beyond Babylon (London: Black Star Publications, 1985) by kind permission of
the Estate of Len Garrison. Sarah 'Rain' Kolawole, poem first published in this
anthology, by kind permission of the author. Marsha Prescod, *Let it Be Told:
Black Women Writers in Britain* (Pluto Press 1987, Virago Press 1988) by kind
permission of the author. Jacob Sam-La Rose, *Breaking Silence* (Bloodaxe
Books, 2011) www.bloodaxebooks.com. Kadija Sesay, *Irki* (Peepal Tree Press,
2013).

All permissions cleared courtesy of Suzanne Fairless-Aitken
c/o Swift Permissions swiftpermissions@gmail.com

Where poets are no longer living, their dates are given.

Contents

Introduction

Ten Poems about Black History guides the reader down the difficult paths of the 1948 Windrush generation's arrival and reception in the UK. It was on 22ⁿᵈ June 1948 that the German-built troopship docked at the Port of Tilbury in Essex, after the first of more than twenty voyages. The Motor Vessel *Monte Rosa*, renamed Her Majesty's Transport *Empire Windrush*, brought service personnel and other Jamaican immigrants to the UK. Between 1947 and 1970, nearly half a million people from the Caribbean left their homes to begin a new life in Britain. The people undertaking this pioneering journey would become known as the 'Windrush' generation.

This cohort of first-generation Caribbean migrants, arriving before the imposition of the 1971 Immigration Act, would face hostility and an unforgiving 'colour bar'. The poetry in this collection responds to that experience. In 'The Hours', Jacob Sam-La Rose imagines a child's perspective on a father forced to work unsociable hours to support his family. Kadija Sesay's 'Streets of Gold' broadens the scope of what was endured in making a living, while the late Jean 'Binta' Breeze offers empathy in 'Mi Duck', blending both dub poetry and North England vernacular. Gritty and harsh realities for post-war immigrants are accentuated by James Berry in 'Revelation' and Kamau Brathwaite in 'The Emigrants [part I] (1967)'.

Marsha Prescod focuses on the resilience Black Britons needed to negotiate a hostile environment in 'Exiles' while Stanley O. Ayodeji's 'Contemplation' offers a moment in which to pause and reflect. Post-Windrush as a new generation born in England negotiated what had become systemically racialised problems; Lenford (Len) Garrison's 'Black Seeds Bring Light' offers a rallying call to the disenfranchised and Sarah 'Rain' Kolawole speaks as the third generation in 'Motherland'. My own poem, 'The Later Stages of Asking Why', suggests how important it is to capture this history and ensure that our stories continue to be told.

Panya Banjoko

Mi Duck

I know I know I know mi duck
I know mi duck I know
I know how England breaks your heart
how summer ends before it starts
I know mi duck I know
I know how cold can shut you in
the blows you've taken on the chin
I know mi duck I know
I know how your lover just walked away
never answered your calls night or day
I know mi duck i know
I know how much you needed love
longed for blue skies up above
for a friend to offer a cup of tea
to sit through the night writing poetry
I know how you long for a child to rock
how you count the ticks on your bodies clock
I know how evening cradles your tears
and how your wrinkles mark the years
I know I know I know mi duck
I know mi duck I know
I know how England breaks your heart
how summer ends before it starts
I know mi duck I know.

Jean 'Binta' Breeze (1956 – 2021)

The Emigrants [part 1] (1967)

So you have seen them
with their cardboard grips,
felt hats, rain-

cloaks, the women
with their plain
or purple-tinted
coats hiding their fatten-
ed hips.

These are The Emigrants.
On sea-port quays
at air-ports
anywhere where there is ship
or train, swift
motor car, or jet
to travel faster than the breeze
you see them gathered: passports stamped
their travel papers wrapped
in old disused news-
papers: lining their patient queues.

Where to?
They do not know.
Canada, the Panama
Canal, the Miss-
issippi painfields, Florida?
Or on the dock
at hissing smoke locked
Glasgow?

Why do they go?
They do not know.
Seeking a job
they settle for the very best
the agent has to offer:
jabbing a neighbour
out of work for four bob
less a week.

What do they hope for
what find there
these New World mariners
Columbus coursing kaffirs

What Cathay shores
for them are gleaming golden
what magic keys they carry to unlock
what gold endragoned doors?

Kamau Braithwaite (1930 – 2020)

The Hours

My other father – the one who stayed –
worked nights when I was a kid.
I never understood nightshifts

although I've pulled them since,
the way the sun comes up like laughter
over your shoulder, some private joke.

Lonely hours, home to all the essential
undesirable occupations that keep the world
ticking over, push it through into another day.

He drove a mail truck up and down the country
and always came back at four or five in the morning –
hours I was only dimly aware of, hours my body

passed through in sleep, like ghost towns
between cities. At first, I slept light, woken
by the sound of his key in the lock, a foreign thing.

Soon, I learned to sleep through.
Some nights I woke when his feet took the stairs,
slow, with care, so as to keep the hour

sacred, undisturbed.

Jacob Sam-La Rose

Streets of Gold

Streets of gold, they promised.

Empty cigarette packets
lined with gold foil,
silver ones too! Generous Britain –
take as much as you like!

Phillip Morris handed us a broom.

Kadija Sesay

The Later Stages of Asking Why

He sits down,
mumbles to himself for half an hour
to see what he can remember,
if anything.

Sometimes he sits for a couple of days
to tease out the memories
of when he started at the old school,
the bruiser teacher once an ex-boxer
who wet his cane to keep it supple,
and then he leans back,
works at remembering something different,
talks about the problem of storing
the past in a head far too full
of making placards.

Why, exactly, did he leave engineering?
If only he could recall
the names that sit on the tip of his tongue.
He tries to write them down,
but stalls, can't remember
why he holds a pad and pen
and scratches his ball-head.

He worked in an office
shared with the caretaker
and the cleaners,
and their rotary disc machines
which harvested dust.

He can see it as if it were yesterday.
Tells himself that names don't matter
and tries to hear the equipment's roar,
or did it hum?

He's done many things since,
travelled the country
with a little bit of money,
he remembers that well.

And the dust, he remembers that too,
dust from the equipment
of dem lickle kin teet bwoy.

He promised himself
he would never forget their names.

If only he could place a finger on the gap
maybe—
if he works hard enough—
anyway,

he went into arts administration,
but can't remember what it was
that made him first stand up

was it the tenth time he was told to go back?
Either way, he decided to clear the dust.

He is certain that he was never alone,
never.

They met in cellars
planning how they might win.

Panya Banjoko

Exiles

Forty years in the factory.
Thirty years on the bus,
Twenty years with machinery,
They don't make them any more like us.

Happy to know which place to go,
Canada, US and Britain,
Whether is canal to build,
War to fight,
Land to till,
We eager to make we heaven.

Small fish in an ocean
Of greed, of gold,
All we dreaming is how to get rank.
So, is families wasted,
An health all gone,
Whilst we putting we lives in the bank.

An when you hear the shout –
We can't get out,
Our pride and spirit get break.
At home prices too high,
An no jobs left to try,
Here,
We is crippled by the Welfare State.

Is a little beer here,
Little dominoes there,
And a lot of funeral to follow.
Having ketch as ketch arse,
Just a pensioners pass,
As a old folks home come tomorrow.

Forty years in the factory,
Thirty years on the bus,
Twenty years with machinery,
Yes...
They don't make them any more like us.

Marsha Prescod

Revelation

Unexpected this arrival,
this face white, not black
like yours, and you come to know
his works, his thoughts, his pains
and pleasures. You see his
home within walls. He has
no wings or receding horizons.

His gestures are the same
little bids that make
his traps equal to yours,
if even his have better
inbuilt swagger
and outward shine.

And you are surprised you can
sort out mountains of words.
You are surprised you
can wonder together, who really
is the governor of boundaries.

James Berry (1924 – 2017)

Contemplation

Sometimes I wonder
As I sit:

Surely *this*
Cannot be it?

Stanley O. Ayodeji

Black Seeds Bring Light

It is not
It is not enough
To show pity
To show hate
To show outrage
To show fear.

It is not
It is not enough
To show guilt
To show despair
To show indifference
To show concern.

It is Time to flush out the
    tears of bitterness and sorrow
It is Time to usher in the new dawn
It is Time to kindle new fires
    and cast new dies.

It is Time to bond love
    into the hearts of men
    It is Time to kindle the spirit
    and empower the soul
It is Time for Black seeds to send new
    roots and bloom fresh flowers
    where there was decay and hopelessness
It is Time for Black seeds to bring
    light into the barren wastes.

Len Garrison (1943 – 2003)

Motherland

Mother,
I answered your call
like an obedient child, I responded
when you called me all battered and bruised,
wanting.

Your home bore holes Mother,
the bombs left craters in your kitchens,
you had no strength to rebuild,
all pitted in scars, your toolboxes empty,

I answered.
Served in the kitchen that I rebuilt.
Mother, you called, and I answered.
travelled from oversea,
to be sent down back alleys,
toward dead ends.

Standing at the back door of your kitchen,
the door I rehinged.
I brought my flame to reignite your fire.
I watched you dine,
my plate remained empty.

You chanted for me to go back home,
but Mother, I stayed,
now at the head of my own table.

Your dutiful Daughter.

Sarah 'Rain' Kolawole